VOYAG

Voyager

PAMELA WILKIE

PETERLOO POETS

First published in 1997
by Peterloo Poets
2 Kelly Gardens, Calstock, Cornwall PL18 9SA, U.K.

A catalogue record for this book is available
from the British Library

ISBN 1-871471-67-2

Printed in Great Britain by
Latimer Trend & Company Ltd, Plymouth

ACKNOWLEDGEMENTS are due to the editors of the following journals: *The Cumberland Poetry Review* (USA), *Gairfish*, *Interim* (USA), *The North*, *Oxford Poetry*, *Poetry Nottingham*, *The Rialto*, *Smiths Knoll*, *Southfields*, *The Spectator*, *The Times Literary Supplement*, *Writing Women*, and the Women's Press anthology *In the gold of flesh*.

'Hit and Run' and 'Doctor X' were finalists in the 1988 TLS/Cheltenham Poetry Competition.

'Facts of life' won 3rd Prize in the Charterhouse Poetry Competition 1991.

'Railway child' was a runner-up in the Kent and Sussex Poetry Competition 1992.

'Joe' was a finalist in the National Autistic Society Poetry Competition 1994.

'Tuareg' won 1st Prize in the *Envoi* Competition 1995.

For Neil

Contents

MORE FAMILIAR TERRITORY

Mutating off Madagascar

Four hundred million years
he's hung out on the ocean floor
and tonight without losing his cool
he looms into your sitting-room,
an eight-foot grey eminence
stirring haphazard fins
in torpid undulations,
trailing the same old boiler-suit
he's worn around the rockface
all these dull millenia.

What brings him up so close,
what has he found down there
glowing in the dark?

By the dug-outs on the shore
the local fishermens' children
curious as lemurs
outstare the fish-eye
of the camera.

Revenant

The deep-frozen bridegroom, fifty years on,
has come down from the mountain, his honeymoon face
unlined, his lips fresh with the kiss he gave
his bride moments before he slipped away
into the jaws of the glacier, and was gone.

The ice snatches and swallows, it cannot digest
but inch by inch there is always peristalsis;
earth's pot is on the boil and the melt is
moving faster into the valley, so the groom
makes haste to join the lovely wife he missed.

Every spring she returns to the crevasse,
kneels at the edge and drops flowers in the place
where he fell. Very soon she will be too old
to climb, nursing her bouquet — her fatherless child —
the light hurting her eyes, her bones sore in the cold.

She's back for the anniversary, on the little train.
In the village they'll smile and nod to see her again —
but someone gently takes her arm and leads her away
through a long white corridor to an icy room . . .
"It's my grandson, bringing me flowers — " is what she will say.

Tuareg

A shimmer coming off the horizon
swathed in the blue of distance
riding out of all statistics.

His language is chiselled from east to west
to stop the words flying off in the wind.
Consonants survive the Sahara.

Admiral of a hundred camels,
salt vessels, he navigated
the routes mapped in his genes.

But the merchandise has all run dry
and famine has left him a skeletal fleet.
The sand road is blurred by wheels.

His day still begins with camels
roaring like Victorian plumbing.
Madame climbs aboard for the morning tour,

the beast proffers its shrivelling stare,
comes within an inch of turning
the lady into a pillar of salt.

Hit and Run

Our wheels edged forward through the village
slithering on tracks of muddied sand.
Twilight, the desert swathed in purple,
instant shadows prostrate before us.

One broke away from the walls and ran out
in front of the car, a child, oblivious.
A scream, not hers, "I'm going to hit her —"
The shock was gentle, humped like a pillow
her body nestled into the mud,
a small figure returning to its clay.

"Is she hurt? I'll take her to hospital —"
Ghosts at the roadside, purdahed women,
covened and flapped in the deepening dusk.
Something moved beside the car
stood wild-eyed between us and them
found a footing on the shifting ground
chose the devils she knew, and ran.

"Is she alright? Is she alright?"
You were out of the car, distraught.
A bystander stirred and shrugged towards us
dismissing your nonsense. "It was nothing.
It was her fault. So let her go."

We were reprieved. The girl ran on
and after her the women, cursing her.
Would she dream that night of falling under our wheels?
Was she used to not knowing what had hit her?
In the dark road a white man was weeping.

Under the Skin

An oasis. A village.
The narrow balcony of an apartment.
Five children, three dark heads, two blonde
bent on improvised manoeuvres with apricot stones.
Brown feet and dusty white ones kick out at the goat
threatening their play.
Teeth flash in laughter.
English giggles erupt. And international imprecations.
Didn't the Arabs invent mathematical calculus? —
small wonder small Europeans are at sixes and sevens.
The battle resolves and will resume tomorrow.
A friendly match.

Unveiled in the house, the darker mother
slips across the passage to her neighbour's door;
"We are sisters under the skin, whatever they say."
A worn, ringed hand gestures to the street
where martial music brays, the military strut
and paper slogans scream.
Branded already by the party watchdog,
the fists on the car, the spitting in the street,
we're mistaken for some other, some unseen oppressor.
Heaven knows they've had their reasons. Fair heads
are fair game. The guns in the alley
wait for the foreign mother . . .

That was years ago. The anger burnt out
in a six-day wonder. The fire went underground.
But now it explodes in the faces of its women,
sears them and shrivels them, consumes them and trashes them
and stuffs them back down the throat of their history
behind the veil, three paces behind the Master —
and Brotherhood is a beast.

Harvest Time in Afghanistan

It could be an Alpine valley,
snowy peaks against postcard sky,
yellow roses round the doors,
vineyards loaded in the sun.

Unfortunately, tending their vines
the local people get both feet
blown off, which makes it hard,
you can imagine, to tread the grapes.

These fields have all been sown
from planes or helicopters —
three million is the estimate,
harvested by women and children.

Yesterday at the hospital
a boy was brought in, aged eight;
he stepped on one, chasing a goat
that strayed, his livelihood.

One leg had gone. The other
hung on by a skein
of twisted muscle at the hip.
Shrapnel through his body.

Today an important visitor,
high ranking in the military,
drops by to see his cousin
slightly wounded in a skirmish.

"Would you care to be shown round?"
Bored with sitting at Headquarters
transmitting distant orders
for the mining of rural areas

he jumps at the V.I.P. treatment.
The doctor knows where to take him —
straight to the children's ward.
Four toddlers are in from play,

one of them has no hands,
the others, well, they're a mess.
The V.I.P. goes silent,
pale, unsteady, a walking cliché.

They continue through the ward.
Nothing said. He fumbles a moment
with his jacket in the doorway —
fifty dollars "for the children."

Counting to 10 in English

The children look forward to showing their father
how they can count to 10 in English.

(Their father, my husband, has been standing
in the killing circle all night long
hooked to the whim of a swinging rope —
their father is made to kneel on the floor,
forced to bite another man's balls —
their father is choking to death on his blood.

These are things I do not know
and no-one here knows how to tell me.)

My husband is a history teacher.
Can I say this in the present tense?

We are most fortunate to be in England,
permitted to stay in this warm room.
We are lucky the caretaker let us in
and kind women bring biscuits and clothing.

We are given wool. We crochet. I am a chemist
in our world. We wait —
                              we wait for news,
and without news we wait for sleep.

The children look forward to showing their father
how they can count to 10 in English.

Reflecting off California

Clashing currents grapple towards the sun
beating the daylights out of this clamorous coast.
The electric ocean sparks, crackles, fissures,
expletes an unmistakable exclamation
that plumes away in the distance. There!
shouldering into view, alive and well,
sharing with us this one wide second
then wheeling below the surface. Our eyes
ache in aftershock — we saw
the Big One on its monumental journey,
the ace in the old globe's deck.

Forgetting for a while the world's children
vanishing at a higher daily rate
than the more popular endangered species,
we're watching by numbers, tagging the survivors,
bad-mouthing the Japanese. And who are we
to begrudge them a few thousand whales?
the sea outstares us, we turn away.

Facts of Life

Nocturnal dustmen of the natural world
since the day before the day of the oldest dinosaur,
they're the same armour-plated mega-survivors

who've hoodwinked us for hundreds of lousy years.
Here's a shiny anglepoise from Madagascar,
those hissing males are heading for a fray —

growing up in Papua New Guinea
one breed suckles its young with TLC,
the world's largest is the West Australian 'rhino'.

Our expert keeps a collection in his bedroom,
"It's lucky, really, I live at home," he says,
"I have a very understanding mother."

In Washington D.C. I ask a child
how many animals she can tell me in a minute —
eyes in the corners of her head she whispers
"Roaches, I jus' sees all dem roaches . . ."

ITALY, FROM TIME TO TIME

Landscape With Old Stone House

The farmhouse lies in thousands of cubic hectares
of Umbrian time.
There is a silence that demands your attention,
pulls you away
from reading in a cool room to stand outside
here at the door
where the hillside leans down its terraces into woodland,
the valley dozes
beneath you, and range after range of drowsy hills
nudge into Tuscany.

From time to time
a finch may shift position in the thicket,
a mile away
in the pasture a horse might mumble on a thistle;
some disturbance
of the air perhaps, as a falling leaf
settles behind you,
a lizard flickers past, or a harvest mouse slips
between grasses.

Listening is not enough, you stare, you scrutinize,
you would touch
the atmosphere if you could, test it with your hand
like a new mattress.
You can't believe that so much landscape and such airways
yield so little sound.

We make no waves here. We could be at anchor
in a legendary sea.

Dust

The house has floors of old country brick
hollowed on the stair by years of boots
plodding through their seasons —
summers of urgent sunlight,
long winter dark in smoky twilight rooms.

Treading slant we walk the decks
of their daily voyages.

Sprinkle, swirl, sweep, and scrub —
still the sugary movement underfoot,
fine flour of terracotta on the hand,
taste of mortality in the breath.

Workmen have been here
with their clouds of undoing.
Grandfather, master-builder, recognised
the writing on the wall
and cursed the skills that choked him.

Down the hillside other men and women
lay three thousand years protected in the earth,
survived an instant, traced in captive dust
when their sanctuaries were opened, then vanished,
shocked after such delay, mysterious as they came,
and held their tongue.

Umbrian Woman, Reclining

She sits, vacant in the vacant yard
on a hard chair, the house behind her,
and stares without seeing towards the road,
listening, not hearing us call; sounding
the depths of her years. Is she trawling
memories of treks in the dawn with her sack
and sickle to haul in grass for her poultry
her rabbits and geese?
                              A walking haystack
we'd see her come from the fields, bent double
but always a hand free to wave.

                              She sits
with hands downcast and her mouth troubled,
lost for the words on her lips to fill
the empty work-space; she leans at an angle
against the wall like an old cart-wheel.

Dear Muriel

I was going to write and tell you

how the goldfinch is turning the handle
of a tune in the fig-tree,

how the siskin squeaks and the serin
mimics a canary, then hisses himself

and the barn-owls hoot the comet
post-marking our valley;

I might have added that springtime
after such snows is quite a miracle,

how the olives came through the freeze-up,
"your" tree as resilient as any,

how the orchids are back, and the hare,
and new calves in the meadow

and the eagle (Bonelli's) is scouting
for lambs on our neighbour's hill;

I'd say, "You should see the wistaria
pouring down the wall!"

But the page is misting already.
You were here just once. That's all.

Lapsus

The snake and I flex our instincts
at the open door. The old stone house
has been in his family since long before
it hosted our summer days.

Transfixed by those basalt eyes
fragmented from these rocks,
I calculate no-man's land —
a second, a split sunlit second.

Saved by the bell of a mule.
A woodman is coming up the track
urging his loaded beast
with intimate curses.

"Mi da una mano?"
Sure! He'll give me a hand
with a stout stick in it. "Ecco!"
The viper stains the ground.

Forget the electric flicker of that tongue,
the live current between us. What remains
is my gauche turning of a phrase,
the chivalry of a man with one arm.

Split Second

Vine leaves in her hair, her roughly garlanded head
hits the ground at speed and rolls, while her torso
gallops on, erect; then one foot slips
from the stirrup and bowing to the inevitable she lolls,
the stump leaking like a war-torn pennant.

Or, in another version, she doesn't lose her head
at all in the vineyard, though her horse, so
mad for the stable that it's all out of step
hell for leather down the hillside, almost falls —
and lurching, she just misses the wire's intent.

Country Ways

We had the builders in,
a three and a half man team —
two on walls,
one on door frames
and the half did window-sills.

With his mid-line view of the world
he was a glossary of door-knobs,
keyholes, taps, underskirts of chimneys.
He could cement you a crawl-space
no other hand could touch.

So when it was time to re-line
the old-fashioned country oven
no questions asked, he stepped up
and vaulted inside.

We left him undisturbed for a couple of hours —
with fresh-picked rosemary
and wild garlic
he was superb.

Wild Life in Rome

From the terrace of the penthouse by the Tiber
to the ground, the only way was in the lift —
one of those cavernous, clanking, open-meshed cages,
carelessly left open at the top, and called down
by some rheumy-eyed old lady dressed in black
who was visiting a friend on another floor.

In the dim light of the passage she finds the handle,
opens the heavy door and steps awkwardly
into the shuddering box, pulls the door shut,
turns, and sees the glitter of its face —
(she had heard of it being walked in the neighbourhood
in its elegant Gucci collar studded with amber
to match the colour of its eyes) — those eyes
staring intently into her own, the saliva
flecked on its lips, the brute whiteness
of its teeth; she breathes the fetid danger on its breath . . .

It was the porter who opened the door, eventually.
The superb creature sprang out and into the darkness,
most exquisitely dressed for a night on the town —
not like the shaggy mimicry of fashionable women
whose furs trail sumptuous mud-flaps round their ankles.

The man did his best with his mop of plenty of chlorine,
but for some days the lift smelled regrettably of cat.

Pizzeria Pagliaccio

Forty-five and harassed by teenage kids
and the structural maintenance of his mid-life wife
and the plaster and the drains of the ancient apartment —
such a snip in the seventies — in the off-centre alley
with the leaning walls and atmospheric street-lamp
which he's grown to resemble,

                               he gangles into work,
head bent forward on a long thin neck, shoulders hunched
like he's biked against the wind —
which he has — and leans into the kitchen,
sticks a finger in a topping, sheds thirty years
and winks at the chef.
                 In limbo for a moment
as he takes off his anorak and fraying jeans
to don the dark trousers and natty red waistcoat —
then a slick of the quiff and he's ready to go on,
to goon and caramba into the dining-room,
pan down the steps and zoom between tables,
loom up on old customers and grumble *che vitaccia* . . .

but give him a bevy of wide-eyed tourists —
he'll swoon for them, moon for them,
clown up and down for them,
six pizzas on his arms he'll tango
and twirl for them, deftly unload for them —
and bow himself out with a music-stand collapse
saved at the last by a grab at the coat-rack,
leaving the scene to the clapping of hands.

che vitaccia what a rotten life

Misapprehended

A dummy steps out from the group by the exit,
there's a tap on your shoulder, a tight-lipped request,
"Excuse me madame, would you come with me please?"

You trail in slow motion past counters of dreamland,
smirking vaguely at shoppers, assistants and mirrors.
Beyond fantasy boudoirs a door marked 'Privata.'

A small, dull room. Talking heads at a table
floating balloons — *Thief! Police! Off with her head!*
You're on dangerous ground in this torrent of language,

losing your balance as concepts rush by you,
with no verb to stand on your present's imperfect,
you drown in opaque declensions of truth.

Diminished, half-naked, your syntax in tatters,
losing sight of the morals you cannot afford,
you empty your purse for a handful of phrases,

'I bring back the sweater — the girl is too busy —
I paid — I am paying — I want to exchange —
I am innocent, ignorant. What can I tell you?'

Preposterous . . . premenstrual . . . immoral . . . insane!
The dictionary's ditched you, you're lost in translation.
There's Justice — in her dark glasses again.

For Her

We have been here before — the elegant skull
caught in the Tuscan light from the arched window,
Renaissance hilltops behind you, a haze over Florence.
You turn towards us with grace as we reach the doorway,
your ivory scalp glinting, the statue alive.
This time you anticipate the fall, you shave your head,
outflanking the chemo's dreary old routine.
Your eyes help us over the threshold. Yes,
we have come, at your invitation — to say goodbye?

You make us welcome, as always, at your table —
and down your pills with style as we sip our wine,
each of us drinking you well in a secret rite.
We smile for His reunion photos — and wonder,
is it a last supper, where everyone knows
what betrayed you? We talk of meeting again . . .
Time to go, down the avenue of cypress.
A last glimpse through a window, a ghost in the glass,
the flicker of a radiance dying away.

Equal in the Eyes of the Birds

are these Italian scarecrows.
Not your rag-clad Giacometti figures
but well-dressed, self-respecting, almost stylish,
some in blouse and skirt,
gracing the estates of well-heeled Tuscany.

In poorer soil, from Friuli to Campania,
scrawny guardians flap their trousered legs.
Call on a tenant farmer, share his meal,
while his woman sits alone in her kitchen,
the smoke, or something, getting to her eyes.

War Artist

"Private Smith!" "Yes sergeant." "You an artist? —
Then paint them number plates!"
His first war-models were army transports
sneaking up from Salerno
to give Jerry a big surprise.

His division surged ahead to Montecassino —
his finest hour, a chance to carry
art history out to safety before the Allied bombing
blew the sanctuary and its saints to kingdom come.

Then the daymares began:
choking on dust and cordite
in the stench and slime of corpses among the monastery ruins;
sketching the boys he knew
charred alive by enemy fire;

forced into the Abruzzi,
the brutal haunted mountains
behind the enemy line, drawing demons while the jeep
lurched between rock-falls and a steeply
guaranteed death in the torrent below.

Never a head for heights,
he fetched up in a military hospital —
delirium, dysentary, diptheria, and a damaged leg.
He painted the shapely nurses. "Birbone!" —
they indulged him, naughty boy.

On to Venice, to purge the city
of fascists with their hands up
surfacing in the canals. No quarter for locals,
the war-sick patriots stamped on their faces
with Allied support.

Fifty years later, a new enemy
with a German-sounding name.
He's outflanked on the home-front; the house has got bigger,
the stairs are unfamiliar, the streets outside unmapped.
And there's a strange woman by his bed.

Night and day have shifted positions.
Should he wave the flag for a truce?
But first get the canvases out! — out of the building,
onto the piazzale, away from the bombers! —
into the fields.

WAVELENGTHS

Saturation Point

This man who wanted to write
about real things (like fulmars
over Beachy Head) lived
surreal disasters; one wife
lost after another
(and in front of the children);
his father moving in
with Alzheimer's;
and coming home one day
to a hard case of arson
including his MS thesis
on the longevity of the cell.

Such raw material,
he barely knew where to begin,
so to clear his mind he set out
on a long sea voyage
on foot, and finally wrote
his epitaph.

It stings like salt spray
in the eyes of his absent friends.

Wavelengths

"Low-level tinnitus," says the consultant.
"An inner-ear condition," he explains.
The patient is devastated. She had thought
the humming she can hear when she lies awake
was the sound of the earth as it turns.

And who is to say that she is wrong?
There are other phenomena to consider.

In the different hours of darkness the shock
that jolts awake the sleeping heart may mark
across the globe, in local time, the moment
when a tremor on a fault starts to crack
the fragile crust, and all Hell breaks loose;

men have mapped their universe with songlines,
gone mad on the imperative of the moon,
eased their anxieties into stones.

Who hasn't been compelled to turn his head
into the sights of an unknown pair of eyes,
some lone marksman in an indifferent crowd?

Twinship, with its preternatural faxes,
sends stark revelations to its own.

But the child who once dreamed the mermaids' singing
now hears the tide forever coming in.

Talent Show

Hydrocephalous little dancer
neatly gyrating on insect limbs,
your ten-gallon head
edgily balanced, like Humpty Dumpty,
on a pint-sized tuxedoed torso —
what possessed your mother to send you to stage school,
dodging the mainstream to learn such tricks?
Did she think in the chorus you'd achieve
elite anonymity, safe in the troupe
of hot-house children chasing the lights?
But all eyes on you, nimble space-chick
who mimics so well the high-kicking line.

So where is the lady to whom you owe everything?
Let her come forward and take a bow.
What modesty's keeping her out of the limelight?
Ah, here she comes now, on to the boards,
featly club-footing it. Give her a hand.

Time Out in the Clock Museum

At first we stood drenched in asynchronous showers
of seconds fleeing the hands of the hours
while the minutes made way for the mass suicide
and anomalous peacocks erupted outside,
before time began beating against the glass
on three hundred different faces and

shepherds and nymphs, gods and goddesses braced
for their bit of the action, wound up for the race
that nobody wins, the sprint to infinity.
Bing! they were off in jingling disunity
from Louis' sopranos to Grandfather's bass
a concatenation of descants, then

without drawing breath the mechanical choir
warped time out of mind as it sounded the hour
over and over, above and beyond
the call of the moment, till rivers of sound
ran down the walls of the room to the floor
and quicksilvered out of the door, but

our ears were in shock and our eyes were too busy
watching the show to see time go missing:
Vulcan was hammering, Cupid was shooting,
ladies were preening and lords were cavorting
in theatres of marble, on platforms of bronze
timeless myths were enacted, until

everything came to a stop. Or a start.
The last chime rang out, the seconds took heart
and returned to their posts in the bedside-repeater,
the pendant, the Empire-regulator,
the carillon bracket, the coachman's alarm,
the compensating pendulum —

and our time was up. The evening tide
would not wait. We joined the peacocks outside
as they trailed their Byzantine thoughts here and there
in the gilded Andalucian air,
and the dance of the hours began over again
in disharmonious clockwork rain,
and the spirits waltzed in Elysium.

Daphne in October

It is autumn I dread most of all,
when I stand out among the crowd.
I hide my eyes in my trembling fingers
to stop the nightmare of his return
assaulting me, the dazzle of his gold,
the rays of his obsession, his mocking face.

In winter he's too vain to try and find me.
He hates the cold. It tarnishes his looks.
So then I'm safe —

                     safe to stand here and dream
of that last springtime, before I heard
those footsteps behind me and I ran
and ran until my lungs would burst —
and all my breath erupted in green leaves
and no sensation in my racing feet
and I stood rooted — while the wind
streamed through my hair, and Apollo's
fury raged on down the hill.

Her Own Person

The raven-lady swerves along her path,
shoulders lunging fiercely down the road,
daring her trolleyful of bags to cut and run.
A sprawl of starlings soars away
discrediting her black flapping cloak.

It's all go — from getting out of bed
on the wrong side of the library step,
rushing her morning prayer — "Oh God oh God" —
shocking the pigeons into disarray
with her short and nasty toilet in the fountain,
then on to her self-appointed situation
minding the store, mumbling over the change,
breaking the street decorum with a roar
of curdled need.

Her life is all wrapped up, but words! — words
clatter about her, get under her feet —
into the gutter with them, let a woman be.

Suffered a mild strobe

under my roof the lights are dimming,
going out in stits and farts —
such a dark blue sigh up there,
night sigh, all those tinkering stars,
they'll fade away if I don't look out.
Where on earth has my lighthouse gone?
I had one once, perfectly good,
but now I suppose I need new lamps.
Trim the wicks, my wicks are tired —
give me the tapers, girl!
don't you know it's light-up time
in my old dome

Not Father's day

He only asked for basic creature comfort,
a gift he hadn't known for half a lifetime,
the warmth of another human body,
a heart beating close in the chilling night.

It should have been so natural, so humane,
something people turn to in extremis —
adrift in an open boat in icy water,
trapped on a high ledge where the air is thin.

"You'd be quite safe you know." Not an easy
thing to say with any dignity at eighty.
Nor could she pretend to be afraid —
his fragile need would hardly be a threat.

Legends ago he might have drunk such kindness
at her breast. But not today. Not now.

Opening Day

Manic staccato barking;
in the stills of dawn a shot
cracks the mist
feathering the hills.

A hoopoe circles the poplar,
crests the look-out station,
swoops to the fig-tree to warn the blackcaps
then bustles into the thicket
to give the red alert:
this is September,
this is war.

The truce ends in the valley,
broken by the sun
blinding down the escarpments.
Dogs will yelp in delirium,
pastel doves will fall,
larks, goldfinch, warblers,
wrens, nothing too small
for the dedicated hunter.

Up on the frontier high road
evacuees line the wires;
this is the last flight out.

"In another September, long before you were born,
there was an awful flutter, such a fearful fuss —
us puttering down misty roads
in the old banger, your mother just four,
right up the coast of France
looking for a ferry, getting the scent of war;
there we were, daft as pheasants
on the wrong side of the wire."

Bird in Hand

Redefining the arc of his free fall
and elegant deflection from the earth,
on through the loop of the swinging lure
with not the slightest loss of feathered face —
though he missed the tidbit spinning in its ogee —
he rides his curve up to the top of a beech
where he stops, instantly nonchalant,
and looks the other way.

But for all his shakings off and deaf ear turning
to the whistled coax, the badinage from ground level,
he is bound by intangible jesses
to the glove of this velvet-spoken, lumpen mammal
who clumps through mud and bramble for a creature
that sees right through him from a thousand feet —
but brings him flecks of a heaven,
bright scraps of illumination from a distant text.

Joe

His hands crab-jump across the carpet,
trying to catch the flickering bait of sunlight.

He scrambles up as you come into the room
and runs right past, and stares at the wall.

Your arms go out to him, "Hello Joe" —
"Hello Joe," is the reflex from his corner.

Born before his time, not quite in ours,
he lives through every day at a tangent.

He'll talk for you — "Good boy. Turn the page."
He'll laugh, he'll climb your knee, he'll bite and spit —

but when he has to sleep alone at night
the lost words flow, seven years down his cheeks.

Cataract

In that fudgy pre-dawn light
furniture dissolves into smudges.
Dark stains shimmy and blurt
out of frame, then suddenly engulf
your foreground with gestures and mouths.

Morning mist lingers on and on.
Fog patches seep into the house,
blunting your rods and your cones.
You begin to feel out of touch.

Walking down the street you're on a ghost-train,
bracing for nasties and the things
that go bump in the day. You wipe
your windscreen till you're blue in the face . . .

Caution! Signals not working. Expect delays.

The Nose

At Grasse in France
in a palace of glass,
in a silent room, louvered and cool,
at a glass-topped desk sits the president
of an academy of phials;
a vast assembly, tinted and stoppered,
tiered in ranks around him.

Behind plate-glass screens
the tourists giggle and call him names:
"Alchemist," they whisper, "magus, sorcerer, wizard,"
this man in his prime, with his elegant suit,
his fastidious profile; no spectacled greybeard
brewing his philtres — but given his calling
he could never encumber his qualification
(his highest degree, his rank and title,
his executive organ) with glasses,
for he is The Nose;
(it sounds better in French).

In a reverse of the usual procedure
his nose earns his pay.
There are deprivations: life's little frissons —
alcohol, smoking, spiced foods — forbidden;
banished from work if he catches a cold;
for he's the supremo, the perfumery's Buddha,
shaman of all this elaborate chemistry,
this lengthy persuasion of essence of petals
in vats and cisterns, pipes and alembics,
these distillations through fats into spirit
(animal fats; it sounds better in Grasse).

A living thesaurus of fragrance and piquance
from damask and jasmine to musk and patchouli,
he's the creator, the olfactory designer

of the custom-made scent, the unique after-glow.
It may take a year to perfect the persona
she will leave in a room, but he offers the client
an aura, a signature sketched in the air,
her own soul in a bottle. Whatever the cost
of this handy transcendence, she'll honour the contract
and pay through
Le Nez.

Doctor X

A clammy man
whose circumspect hands have been around
too many cold limbs.
Decorously he works within the law
as, distantly, he walked along the wards.
Do not ask him to vouchsafe
anything beyond the appropriate medication
or the relevant referral.
Do not expect him to laugh
at your death-defying little jokes
or to encourage chat about the weather
in the clinic's sterile zone.
You're here for the examination; pass or fail,
it's immaterial to him.
Never mistake him for a Doctor of Divinity
or Philosophy or other alternative medicine.
He studied at a very eminent School
and Affability was not an option.
Not like your red-blood universities of life.

MORE FAMILIAR TERRITORY

My War

1. HOME GUARD

Sticky perforated paper covered our windows
like dirty lace curtains, gluey views;
a home-grown wall appeared in front of the kitchen
where Mum washed up with the daylight through the peepholes.

But the magnum opus was halfway down the garden,
Dad's great earthwork. For weeks he spaded a hole,
slippery steps down to a muddy pool,
slimy walls rising up to my ears.

On week-end leaves Dad dug, a backyard Hercules,
spectacles steaming. He never admitted defeat —

but when the bombs fell two streets away
(and Dad was somewhere secret inventing radar)
we went over the road to Mrs. Brown's cellar,
Mum, me in my siren suit, Teddy in his.

The next morning Mum was out in the garden
digging potatoes. I jumped in the hole to play.

Years after, I picked the scabs of wartime off my window.

2. SPECIAL FRIEND

He would send me secret messages from the spare room,
trilling his dots and dashes across the landing.
I'd pretend to understand his coded games
and show off with my fluent S.O.S.

He came to stay for a time in our back bedroom,
a quiet, soft-spoken foreigner with one suit
and a small attaché case full of tricks —
like the toilet-bag with an aerial and no toothbrush,
the little gun among his socks and hankies.

He had 'such nice Continental manners,' said my mother.
He kissed her hand politely, praised her cooking,
showed us pictures of his tall fair-haired sisters.

'It's the husband you feel sorry for,' said the neighbours
shaking their heads and looking down the road,
'being in the Forces and away at the War.'

The lodger left all of a sudden after tea-time
just as it was getting dark outside.

He jumped that night from a small plane into Norway.
They shot him while I was playing in Kindergarten.

Railway Child

Bemused at four years old
I would watch my father playing trains
on my behalf,
first laying out the rails
linked in twos along the floor
(linoleum was best, the carpet snagged the locos,
fluffed up the works,)
then the engines, green Great Western,
red for the raw North East;
next the coupled coaches, (we took for granted
that their tinny interiors were bustling with life,)
and lastly the guardsvan, where of course
the little man with the flag
would wave and blow his whistle —
but never when we were watching.

The iron road outgrew the sitting-room,
skirting-boards were scratched and battered
by runaway rolling-stock.
My mother's edict banned the network
from the house —
Pamela's trains must go outside,

to be rehabilitated, overhauled, extended, doubled, trebled
through looplines, crossings, junctions, wayside halts and termini
in the garage.

I followed them,
and perched in polite acknowlegement
on the bonnet of the car,
sniffing grease and sawdust, the sparky smell of electricity
as express trains raced around me
up and down the lines on their custom-built shelving,
clattering into signals, shunting off to sidings,
ferrying tiny passengers

from Bangham to Crashup-on-Lyne,
with a change at Great Puffington Junction.
If I'd turned my head more quickly I'd have seen them go aboard,
they were there, just out of eyeshot,
commuting through their lives,
risking spectacular derailments and tremendous impacts,
but never mechanical failure,
not with Dad in charge.

Physicist at Play

in memory of F.G.S.

The frisson of writing his initials
finds my fingers' blood-memory
retracing the way he wrote

at that neo-Gothic desk
where his oscilloscopic pen
jagged across the paper

as he analysed the elusive matter
of the theatre,
                a predilection in the genes
by osmosis, his Stratford forbears
snug in the church with William.

Performing experiments in the lab
he was always 'Bill' — the Warwickshire lad
gifted with a theory of acting
that made an Oh! of our little town.

Old Habits

My Etruscan mother hid the face
in her mirror, powdered over the glass
as they used to do, out of respect
for the newly dead. We must never catch their eyes . . .

She forgot the dressing-table's triptych spies
that followed her shadow in the room. By neglect
she met her own perdition in its maze,
an image to consume her dying days.

Absence

When you are not here
the house makes subtle noises,
shifts uneasily in its joints
like an elderly woman clenching
and unclenching her hands;
there's a non-specific tapping,
a heightened heartbeat somewhere in the structure
between joist and beam, iron and restless wood.

I understand. I too am testing the foundations,
sensing the unbalance, gauging the stress.

The Other Valentine

My true love hath my heart, and you are he —
but there's another who became a part of me
on a London street last night. He looked like you
in the rainy light, half-lying, as you do
under the blanket when you're first awake
not wanting to disturb me, ready to take
off and bring coffee — no demands,
no special pleading, no outstretched hands.

We could be meeting in a room of books,
talking face to face. Instead he looks
apologetic, out of place on the pavement, hurled
off-course by the vectors of this world.
And I apologize too, to stop the platitude
rising to his lips, the terrible gratitude.

Distance Vision

(for Alexa)

At the new moon of your birth I wished
for you a life without delusion.
Any mother for any daughter
might do the same; a wish that reaches
past the stars.
                    I could not see
what light-years from the real world it was,
and that I of all your universe
would be the most inconstant.

The Moment

(for Max and Mette)

The air was textured with music,
ruffled with expectation;
the white light in the chancel began to stir and shift
from the pale stone of the altar, the radiance of brass,
the opal glow of roses pillowed in their heather;
the light edged away
and with it the turning of heads
to the gentle country commotion of a carriage at the door;
a pause, the checking of heartbeats —
and then, like the spring
after the long disbelieving of a Scandinavian winter,
she was there, she was the rose,
she was the fortune of the heather,
she was all the sunlight,
and her smile moved us on
into summer time.

Voyager

for a grandson

We seem so close,
like a pair of skaters round our pond.
From your one year
to all of mine,
no distance really.

But now you must go home —
thousands of miles.
How can I smile so wide
and wave enough
for such a leaving?

Worlds apart, my words
and your perceptions.
Innocent of past or future,
you cannot know
that you are going to forget me,
your infinite, engrossing Now
rises like valley mist between us —

you must travel further
than tomorrow,
you have to navigate all the years it takes
to grow and discover what I mean
by my secret tears at the gate.

Hubbled

It's Sunday and I'm searching for God
in the Review Section under Science.

Last night I was under the stars
and I zeroed out in a snowstorm of O's,

and our planet just one more snowflake held
in a child's hand for a minute until it melts.

Monkey Business

The bright-faced lemurs, like exhilarated boys
who front the air as they leap into the pool,
launch across chasmic distances between trees,
their limbs outstretched to embrace the gift of flight,
ruddered and ballasted by rippling tails.

Among these airborne primates there's a strain
who have no tails — they still make mighty bounds
of thirty feet or more, but backwards.
What purpose this fulfills is not quite clear.

As we watch our new generation, six-month wonder,
self-propelling across the carpet, in reverse,
while the shining toy diminishes in his sights
and a small but ugly cataclysm threatens,
the suspicion grows, is Evolution wearing off?